# this
# second
# layer.

words by Christine Jessica

# THIS SECOND LAYER

Copyright © 2017 by Christine Jessica. All rights reserved. Printed in the United States of America. No portion of this book may be used or reproduced without written permission except in the case of reprints in the context of reviews.

www.rosesinsoho.com

ISBN: 978-0692939086

"you tried to peel away my skin, but you reminded me I have a second layer."

-

*poetry and prose written by Christine Jessica*

# INTRODUCTION.

*hello*, again.

you stared me down as if you assumed to never see my face on another occasion. I know love and lust were the only two emotions of your soul – yet, you cracked a smile. sometimes, I found myself contemplating which was the one for me.

I rehearsed your following question in my mind on numerous occurrences. you pondered, why *did* you actually leave me that time? was it the way my words felt like a knife to your throat, snipping off threads of your sweater like lumberjacks do to trees? the possibilities seemed endless, and that left me on edge. a jump, so high, that the ground looked like cloudy pillows. a made-up fortress of ease, where I think you had run away to. you felt a questioning sense of security, as I was ready to fall, once more.

I landed in your arms in the moment I was supposed to hit the ground. I expected red blood to splatter, but it was only my favorite color of roses, softly brushing against my feet. your apologies always felt like freshly cut stems, placed delicately in water. I found myself in an ocean.

without any concerns, you taught me how to swim. there would be no waves in my lungs, this time. you allowed me to believe that I was actually floating, while you were holding me up with a life vest. a part of me had to know it was impossible, as I pretended it was the least you could do. you tried to peel away my skin, but you reminded me I had a second layer. on some level, you were aware of how frequently you had vanished on me.

but, my dear, you had never left. you are not even here anymore, and I am still talking to you. content? possibly. losing my mind? without doubt.

I woke up from the dream, and you were as gone as our love. the love, from Forever Ago.

*goodbye*, again.

Christine Jessica.

THIS SECOND LAYER by Christine Jessica

MAY IS HERE.

I rely on picking petals off
in order to tell if you love me or not

maybe if we spoke in flowers,
I'd be able to understand
why we're falling apart

## BUSY STREETS, CROWDED SIDEWALKS.

this is an ode to the man I will love.

I know you're out there somewhere. maybe you aren't waiting for me like I am waiting for you, but I know the day will come where you will see me and ultimately fall in love. perhaps, not in a field of flowers, but standing on a street corner while the taxi swaying past riles up my skirt and I have to tame it. maybe you're inhaling the smoke of your first cigarette, and there's a strange presence in your conscience that has the same voice as mine telling you to stop. the universe might have you now, but I will have you soon.

I used to be afraid of being alone, until I realized that I am no longer. I will have you by my side. I will find you, someday – along these busy streets and crowded sidewalks. until then, I will fall in love with me.

## DISASTER.

*you've ruined me,* I stated. *you've fooled my current world into thinking there could be someone better than you.*

*not only that, but you made me believe that this is the worst thing that could happen to me. you caused a disaster that is no more than a wicker flame on a candle.*

I breathed in the air that once felt like fire.

*it doesn't even reach the room.*

## LIVING IN A DREAM.

he looked at me and spoke
words around my neck,
humming a slender melody
that laced across my ears

*what am I to you?*

leaning in for a kiss,
softer than rabbit's fur
yet, one that hit me
like a slap to the face

I felt something beating inside me, for once,
I knew I had a heart
but it was just in hiding

*my blue-eyed dream boy,*
*that's what you are*

*THIS SECOND LAYER by Christine Jessica*

WHEN LIFE HANDS YOU LEMONS.

I look at you in a different light
since I can't find the old one

and with such a sour note
you left this on,

I will make lemonade

A STORYBOOK ENDING.

I see a path up ahead

for us to walk down

we both want to be right,

but one of us must go left in this lifetime

otherwise, we will never cross paths again

*THIS SECOND LAYER by Christine Jessica*

LITTLE THINGS HURT THE WORST.

*kiss my cheek.*

*no,* you paused. *nose, neck, hands.*

I began to wonder –
did I fall in love with you,
or did I fall in love with
what you made me out to be?

## DIVE.

I am found in deep water,
I never knew how to float before you

I'm swimming through the pain,
waiting for you to take a dive

if I take your hand
and pull you under,

will your heavy heart
make you sink?

*THIS SECOND LAYER by Christine Jessica*

SUAD.

I know you want me to remain
a caterpillar forever,
but I am already
a butterfly

and if you try to rip off my wings,
I know how to sew
and if you try to step on my dreams,
I will only fly away

IN A RUSH.

I feel a beat,
shifting inside of my chest –
except,
there is no heart

only a large, ticking clock
counting down the days
and hours
and minutes

of how much time I have left
on this Earth

and I know I am young,
but I want love now

so, where is he

or, rather, where did he go

*THIS SECOND LAYER by Christine Jessica*

REGRET.

to pass you in a car,
and find out much too late

to slip in time,
and fall right out of it

to have her voice be your favorite,
and hollow out mine

to be in love,
and make it my deepest secret

LAST SUMMER.

we were laying on a bench when I felt your hand reach over to hold mine. I felt at home, although it was miles away.

we had the most perfect view of the sunset overhead. the mere thought of closing my eyes reminded me that my dreams could not prepare me for someone like you.

I know I fell in love with you last summer -

maybe you fell in love with me while I wasn't looking.

*THIS SECOND LAYER by Christine Jessica*

## WHAT'S STOPPING ME?

tips of tongues

bottoms of lakes

white butterfly kisses

yellowjacket stings

mother's wound

father's fist

botanical gardens

cemeteries

today, I finally realized

I am separate from the boy

who tried to ruin me

MANNEQUINS.

I think I'm going to see you
everywhere that I go,
because my brain is already
picturing your hands
on the window shop mannequins
I'm passing by on this city street

and I begin to wonder
if they are a perfectly delicate match to mine
when held up in comparison

so, you placed your right thumb
on top of my left
and we found two similar beauty marks
mirroring each other

maybe it shows the pinpoint
of where we met in another life

## CHERRIES.

I glanced at an old Polaroid of us,

it belonged on the corner

of my writing desk

months ago

I don't know how fond memories

are becoming so distant,

how the colors are fading

from warm to dull

like I won't remember

anything, soon

even red lipstick

leaves a mark on your skin

when you try to wipe it off,

and you're left with

a cherry stain

*THIS SECOND LAYER by Christine Jessica*

## THE WEATHER OUTSIDE. – haiku

he has a calm face

but one that could end large storms

and make them minor

THIS SECOND LAYER by Christine Jessica

## DO YOU LOVE?

it was the last day of Summer in the daylight of his apartment. he grabbed me by my wrist as he said, *"don't close your tired eyes yet. we have a lot of staying up to do."* it wasn't about the endless feeling, either – it was about the enormous amount of comfort that I found in his arms.

I had no clue what being cared for felt like, but I believed it was present the moment he first laid his mind against my skin. carefully, I intertwined my fingers with his until an imaginary *click* had sounded. there was a glow in his eyes, but I couldn't tell if it was the cause of the rainbow on his bedroom wall (maybe it was just from the mirror). I wished that I could make him forget it all. I knew I would give him rest.

he poured one cup of coffee and forgot about the second, as he was not used to the company. as I brushed my teeth with his toothbrush, I thought of the word *home*. I liked the sound of that.

I believed it was my turn to grab him by the wrist and ask him a simple question. *"do you love?"*

the hardest part was the moment before an answer.

## MAYBE IT WAS.

maybe it was the way
you called me sunshine,
maybe it was the way
you showed me light,
or maybe it was the way
you taught me to love myself –

but I loved you so hard,
I don't know how my heart
hadn't split into two.

*THIS SECOND LAYER by Christine Jessica*

THIS IS WHERE I'LL LEAVE YOU.

at the corner shop,
where you bought me a snack
and asked me for my name

at the smile that appears
on the lines surrounding your mouth,
even though it suits you nicely

at the picture of an old dog,
and even if it cannot learn new tricks,
it will learn to love again

at the back of my mind,
in the left vein on my hand,
and the right side of my heart

## CAT'S CRADLE.

I feel like you are still holding onto
your end of the string,
even thousands of miles away

I am still,
watching the string wrap around my body
as it tightens and hits my veins

losing circulation
until I can hear
your heartbeat enveloping mine

this red rope of thread
is swallowing me whole

and while I am wanting you to hold on

I need you to let go

## THIS SECOND LAYER by Christine Jessica

FRANCESCA.

I remember coming back
from a long drive with my father
after vacation

he would say,
*we're almost home*

I find myself saying that
as I'm walking towards my love
with open arms
and widened eyes

you were my house
but it's like you've never left

*THIS SECOND LAYER by Christine Jessica*

A SUN DAY.

the room became muggy
and I was able to peel away
the frayed, dark wallpaper
to reveal a much more soothing tone

I began to wonder,

why do we hide ourselves
only to please others,
when the sun is shining
and baby birds know how to fly

## THIS SECOND LAYER by Christine Jessica

I AM HERE.

I had arrived in your driveway at five. it took some time to muster up the courage to ring your doorbell and confess my feelings for you. *what do I need to do in this situation?* do I get down on my knees and beg for you to fall in love, or do I give you a sucker punch to the face? at that point, I wasn't sure which would heighten my survival rate. I looked at the doormat underneath me as I rehearsed my words.

*you can be you around me, there is absolutely nobody else to be. I know love has the ability to bring pain, but maybe ours will only be from lip bites and sleepy legs.*

*your eyes shine my favorite light, almost like the sun is still highlighting the sky while there aren't even stars present. I must have been out here for a while.*

*I am always just a knock-on-wood away. so, I am standing outside of your door – please, let me in.*

little did I know, you were smiling down from your second-floor window and listening.

*"the door is already unlocked for you."*

## THIS SECOND LAYER by Christine Jessica

BETWEEN.

you need her

and I need you

but that's okay

because this poem

is written about

two different people

(his love feels a little different,

I guess that's what I traded in for)

*THIS SECOND LAYER by Christine Jessica*

A STORM.

I told you my love
was good and borrowed,
endless seas to drown
every sorrow,
I told you holding my hands
were so far from sin,
they'd have your skin peeling
though pale and grim,
I told you my needs
were different from yours,
I throw back the starfish
even if washed up on shore,

I told you I'd be here
as long as you stayed,
but you had already left
as the sky above me grayed

## SUNSHINE.

*how do you know you love him?*
you asked.

*because I can still say his name*
*while containing the sun in my eyes,*
*even though I have seen the night.*

*THIS SECOND LAYER by Christine Jessica*

WHEN FIRST LOVE ENDS.

I wrote about you
like there was never an ending

written with a fountain pen
that never smudged,
even though I am left-handed

so, if she makes you hurt,
don't come crawling back to me

this was *your* choice
*you* decided to leave

(just because I gave you light,
don't expect it to stay on)

*THIS SECOND LAYER by Christine Jessica*

NOT HEARTBROKEN.

is it still called
a broken heart
if you have glue
to fix it yourself

not heartbroken –
just learning to love
on my own

*THIS SECOND LAYER by Christine Jessica*

LEILA.

I think

once you take

a bite

of the real world,

you'll have

a taste

of me

I've only stolen

one beat from your heart,

you still have millions to go

*THIS SECOND LAYER by Christine Jessica*

BLUE SKIES ARE CALLING.

a love letter left on a picnic bench
in the park you first held his hand
and kissed him goodbye

an elderly man who yelled at you
for stealing the spot on the bus next to him
that he saved for his wife

a person kneeling on the sidewalk,
proposing to their significant other
while you were only passing by

maybe this is not *your* moment –
but it is somebody's.

*THIS SECOND LAYER by Christine Jessica*

ONE DAY LATER.

*Sunday nights are made for missing you*

I bury my face in your diary,
so I can feel close to your skin again

I feel something missing from my bed,
like the outline of an apparition

I turn my pillow over to its cold side,
I was so used to seeing you do the same

*but it'll soon be Monday*

*THIS SECOND LAYER by Christine Jessica*

POINTING TO THE SKY.

I have always looked up when we were together –

I guess I should have known
the sky looked too much like mud
to be able to hold a Heaven.

now, I realize I was hanging upside down.

*THIS SECOND LAYER by Christine Jessica*

A SCENE IN A COFFEE SHOP.

it was a strange kind of morning,
one that didn't hurt

you came back to me in ways
that I couldn't imagine

it was real, this time,
not a movie scene in a Hollywood coffee shop –
no lights, no cameras,
and if there were people,
I couldn't notice

multiply our past love by ten tons
and you will get our end result

*THIS SECOND LAYER by Christine Jessica*

KEEP YOURS.

I believe people are like promises

we both break, eventually

maybe some faster than others

but we all go in vein

so, tell me,
will you leave or die first?

*THIS SECOND LAYER by Christine Jessica*

DO YOU WANT TO HEAR A SECRET?

I learned the word *heartbreak* at a young age.

I went to a park, holding the hand of my mother, and watched a teenager fall off his skateboard. it taught me to wear kneepads.

I saw my best friend's parents move into separate apartments. I didn't understand, at first, why I'd be dropped off at her mother's one day, and her father's the next. it taught me that happy people live together.

when I was the age of a new adult, I "accidentally" wound up in a bar. I sat next to a drunken man, who didn't stop consuming gin from the moment I had got there. it taught me to be careful.

*heartbreak.* I never thought I'd be able to understand how that feels. I had all of the answers. I wouldn't allow it, because I was invincible. but, oh, I do. I do now.

I wish I was wearing kneepads on the day you broke my heart.

*THIS SECOND LAYER by Christine Jessica*

## THE ANSWER WAS RASPBERRY.

he tasted like lemonade,

I think that's what he was drinking before we kissed

it was Summer's end when he left me,

three days passed by

and it was September,

when he belonged to you

do his lips remind you of lemonade now, too?

raspberry,

strawberry,

or just plain lemon,

you tell me

I'm guessing you're just greedy enough to get the kiss

and not pay attention to the flavor

*THIS SECOND LAYER by Christine Jessica*

ALONE, NO LONGER.

you're gone now

no more heartbreak,
no more sound –
I could get used to this silence

who is there to scold
who is there to fight
who is there to judge

I only have to fend for myself

you're gone now

but the world seems a little larger
and my eyes are a little wider

I think I can rock *myself* to sleep at night

## NINE P.M.

I have looked Death in the eye,
and withheld a conversation;
*I think you'll need more than you imagine.*

but when you imagine it all,

a house into a home
a pair of hands into a human
a heart into a nest
a darkness into a light switch
a bullet into a target

what are you supposed to need?

*THIS SECOND LAYER by Christine Jessica*

SNOWFALL.

a drop of snow

landed on my tongue,

a grasp of innocence

as my taste buds sprung,

I closed my mouth

to take it in,

another drop placed

on the tip of my chin

this piece of snow

reminded me of you,

I think that's why

it once loved me, too,

I knew from the start

how emotions felt –

the speck of white,

in quick succession, would melt.

*THIS SECOND LAYER by Christine Jessica*

## DOPAMINE.

*if love is just a chemical reaction*

the odds are against you for winning the lottery
trash is another man's treasure
sugar weakens your teeth
we lose before we gain
cars can crash into you while you're not moving
babies expected to know their place in the world
we cry over stolen items and not stolen people
even a knot can be untied

*why do I need it so badly*

## YOUNG ENOUGH TO KNOW BETTER.

all of these photos of you

scattered around my bed

remind me of the time you told me,

*you're still so young*

like I didn't know what love was

I'm now 29 years old,

and looking at the ring on my finger

and child in my arms –

I'm reminded of why you left

*THIS SECOND LAYER by Christine Jessica*

A DEEP BREATH.

I have done so much

for people

who do not appreciate

my presence

now I must

do so much

for me.

*THIS SECOND LAYER by Christine Jessica*

IT ALMOST FELT LIKE LOVE.

he said he would take me to Paris,

I told him I'd pack our bags

he said he would take care of my heart,

I told him I'd move my ribcage out of the way

he said he would lead me when there's a roadblock,

I told him I'd walk with my eyes closed

he said he would spend life with me,

I told him I'd plan the days

as he swallowed his words,

I knew there was a difference –

I guess, sometimes,

you can say things without any meaning

*THIS SECOND LAYER by Christine Jessica*

POWER.

even with this hate,
there are things that I love –

this pen,
this paper,
this head on my shoulders

the rose's shape before it blooms,
French sweets,

you.

AT THE TRAFFIC LIGHT.

every busy street
has at least two ways to turn

I was foolish for not thinking
you'd go left
when things weren't right

## DREAM WORLD.

my heart is so big
and my bones are so little,
but I am not letting lost love
weigh me down

I can build myself up
like a tower
and protect my insides
with thicker foundation

I used to imagine a dream world
where nothing could hurt me,
but now, this is a dream
I am experiencing awake

I made this land on my own,
and that doesn't faze me;
what's a queen without her king?
*powerful.*

*THIS SECOND LAYER by Christine Jessica*

WHEN.

when I love,
I love hard

as a rock,
if you insist-

so, tell me,
when there's a boulder in the road

will it block my way?

POSSIBILITY.

you could give him your heart
and beg him to love you,
but he still has to fall in love
with something deeper than skin

you could wear a wedding band on your finger
and treat him like he is the world,
but he would have gained love
and you would have gained a loss

*THIS SECOND LAYER by Christine Jessica*

EVERY LAST BIT.

a *hello*

we smiled with our eyelids
with nervous kiss
and first touch

I slept next to you
with the person you were then
and the person you are now

we shared secrets
with drunken lips sewn together
and the stars glued on the ceiling

a *goodbye*

## ORIGAMI.

I found my love letters to you
my words were once so beautiful
now, I can only spell out *hurt*

so today, I will take my time
to fold them into paper cranes

because everything can turn
into something good, once again
if you let it

SKELETON.

let it go, if it's eating you alive

because he doesn't deserve
to rattle your bones

if he isn't the one
that found a way
to put them together

## IF IT DOES.

no matter what happens,

if this works out, or doesn't,

I want to thank you for everything

you made me realize

I was invincible instead of invisible,

you made me long

for something I could never dream of,

you made me see

how wonderful of a person I truly am,

you made me feel

like I was actually living

and, if it does,

thank you for that, too.

*THIS SECOND LAYER by Christine Jessica*

LONG GONE.

I can't blame you for changing your mind

but when I look into his eyes,
they will be blue.
when you look into her eyes,
they will be black.

maybe, in that moment,
you will realize I cannot be replaced.

*THIS SECOND LAYER by Christine Jessica*

WATCH ME.

it was all about you at one point,
I believe that's how I got lost

you never noticed my love

until you watched it
walk out the door

and fall into the arms
of a person that makes life seem fifty-fifty,

equal shades of black and white

the moon with some stars

milk and cookies

as that is how love should be

*THIS SECOND LAYER by Christine Jessica*

AFTER ALL.


I think you'll find a piece of me

in the bouquet of roses

held by your left hand

at her front door


soon, the petals picked for her

will freshly turn

and fade away


similar to how you loved me at one day,

and disappeared at one night


and red is my favorite color,

after all

*THIS SECOND LAYER by Christine Jessica*

## THIS IS MY TURNING PAGE.

I put your favorite book away
and stored it underneath my bed

I kept it out, in case you visited,
but it seems less likely by the day

I think you loved me
when you held my hand,
but do you remember
when you asked me to let go?

I feel that books like this
should always be left open

(but I can write my own story now)

*THIS SECOND LAYER by Christine Jessica*

I WISH IT WASN'T.

don't tell me it wasn't real

anything that feels

like money strapped to a bomb,

like Winter without the thought of Spring,

and, especially,

like an ache in my heart

that will not seem to fade –

is more than fantasy

*THIS SECOND LAYER by Christine Jessica*

SHOOT.

you see,

my sadness is solely based off

your loaded lies

it's a shotgun held up to my skull,

threatening the purity of my brain

and I am staying in place,

waiting for you to pull the trigger

or, maybe, I'm *begging* you to

*THIS SECOND LAYER by Christine Jessica*

MY EYES.

I think my eyes looked at you
with hope that you'd say a few words:

*stay,*

*love,*

*always*

instead, they saw you walk away

and, just like that,
you were gone before
you even showed up

*THIS SECOND LAYER by Christine Jessica*

HIDE AND SEEK.

you face the other way
when I walk in the room,
like you don't know what's good for you

or, maybe you do,
and your heart is just in hiding

do I have to go find you,
or will your wandering eyes
bring you back home?

*THIS SECOND LAYER by Christine Jessica*

NOW THAT YOU KNOW.

everybody has something to tell

with alcohol on their breath
or coughing up a lung,
pillowcases that haven't been washed
since their love had left,
phone calls that ring
as the receiver leaves them on silent,

but, sometimes,
they would rather *not*.

*THIS SECOND LAYER by Christine Jessica*

NIGHT. – haiku

you made me realize

I was brighter than sun

when my thoughts were night

## WHAT ELSE?

you fell in love

with the moonlit sky

the touch of our hands

the rooftop on our backs

the airplane flying overhead

the whistling of the wind taking shape

the never-ending pattern of stars

just not with me

WHILE YOU GO.

I could breathe without you,

even if my heartbeat is a little too fast.

I could feel without you,

and, at times, a little too much.

I could see without you,

although my eyes might be half open.

the thing is,

I know I do not want to.

that is how I am so sure.

*THIS SECOND LAYER by Christine Jessica*

DEAR: WOMEN.

teach your daughters to love,

to hold each other's hands when they are scared,

to fight with their fists and over their hearts,

to look both ways before crossing the street,

to move on after a breakup,

to cook your favorite meals,

to use their voice loudly,

to stick up for what they believe in

not, just because, boys can -

because girls are capable

of more than what they are told

*THIS SECOND LAYER by Christine Jessica*

## GONE, FORGOTTEN.

*I think I forgot about you*

I woke up this morning
to find out the pain had left me,
I am outliving the once impossible

I met a handsome boy in the city,
he chopped his hair off
and put the remnants into his sincerity

he followed me to his car and we went on a long drive

I was hypnotized, seeing the road trailing backwards
through the side mirror,
as he asked what was bothering my head

nothing is now, I mean that completely
*and it's beautiful*

*THIS SECOND LAYER by Christine Jessica*

IT WAS PROBABLY NOTHING.


the moment I knew

I had lost you


was the moment

I reminded you

to love me.

BEDSHEETS.

I leaned my head against the other pillow
and my bedsheets were still caressed
with the outline of your silhouette,
and I couldn't stop thinking how
you didn't say a word to me,
no matter how hard you tried

I don't like fighting until the sun's up
there's always beauty in the rise
but we seem to miss it every chance
as our tired eyes shut
and my thoughts begin to race
about how much *I love you*
*I can't let you go*
*I need you to stay*

I was dreaming about you again, wasn't I

*THIS SECOND LAYER by Christine Jessica*

LOVED.

for the first time in my life

I feel loved

by my friends

my parents

my sister

my teachers

my pet

just not loved by you

and that's okay

because that would mean one person

compared to plenty

I will not screw this up

*THIS SECOND LAYER by Christine Jessica*

## WHO ARE YOU?

you promised a forever

I know that I promised my love
would be forever, too,
but there is a difference here

I feel like I'm truly becoming myself
while you're becoming someone else

I am sticking up and moving on
and loving every bone in my body
and all of the hairs on my head
and the teeth in my mouth
and the future in my eyes

so, while you spend time looking in the mirror
and not knowing who you are,
I pass one by
and know who I am

## THIS SECOND LAYER by Christine Jessica

SPARKS.

our love didn't shoot off fireworks
or catch fire of the tallest trees

it was just a calm quiet,
a sound I wouldn't mind growing old to

now that you're gone,
I look up at the night sky

and wish every single day was the Fourth of July

*THIS SECOND LAYER by Christine Jessica*

TELL ME.

I taught myself how to ride a bike,
feeling invincible as I'm a threat
to the gravel underneath me,
with my father aside

I taught myself that I was left-handed,
as my sister would put crayons
in my right, and I'd refuse
like it was poison

and I taught myself how to love,
but not in the way of loving you

so, tell me a reminder
of how I can go on,
just like I was able to before I knew your name

*THIS SECOND LAYER by Christine Jessica*

SANDALWOOD.

playing his favorite songs on repeat

so I could remember the words,

always fixing that one piece of hair

that reaches past his eyebrow,

setting our watches at the same time

to beat at the exact tempo,

buying a new perfume

as his new obsession was sandalwood,

allowing him to wrap me up in velvet

although, I hated the feeling,

buying dark chocolate at the grocery store

so I could learn the meaning of *bittersweet*,

I loved him like no one ever will

DISTANT.

you started spending nights with me
instead of days –
I could only be found in your dreams

like a ghost, trapped in four corners,
I had the ability to leave, if it was my goal

a bullet, lodged
in a frail poet's chest

you're *sorry*,
you're *sorry*,
well, so am I

I've become like you,

distant

*THIS SECOND LAYER by Christine Jessica*

## THREE SUGARS, PLEASE.

you were always the one to remind me that small things are mistaken in large packages. it was always quality over quantity, too – I even did this to my coffee.

"*you should try cane sugar,*" you whispered across my ears in a mute café. "*not that bleached stuff. it's better for you.*"

this caught me in memory of your tangents, how you would rant about seemingly meaningless things. to your surprise, they were never redundant to me. I could sit there, with my hand resting on my chin, for hours.

catching my brain in the past, I looked over at the vacant chair parallel to me. I watched my fingers reach over to the sugar jar and fumble around for a few. it seems that this café didn't know of you.

I felt the room getting dimmer, with every bleached sugar packet I opened.

*THIS SECOND LAYER by Christine Jessica*

A CHOICE.

I once held onto your arm
like you were my security blanket
and I was three again

I know that our love was pure,
and I wish I could still call it that now

I used to trace the back of your hands
like it was a sheet of connect-the-dots
and I was seven again

love is very patient, but I am not a waiting game

I kissed you on a Saturday evening for the first time
like I was stuck at a party, playing spin-the-bottle
and I was twelve again

I don't hate you, nor did I give up on you -
I am choosing to let you go
because I am in love with you

THE KEY TO YOUR APARTMENT.

I think if we ripped our hearts
out of our chests,
they'd fit together like lock and key

but not even that is forever

locks could be broken into
and keys could snap in half

and I think I see noon at my doorstep

or, maybe, it's just you ringing the bell

*THIS SECOND LAYER by Christine Jessica*

## THE ONE WITH YOU IN IT.

I've experienced two kinds of lives -

a wallet filled with train tickets
film cartridges kept aside
empty water bottles in the backseat of a car
fabric scraps thrown in trash bins
*the one, where I had everything*

a bathrobe, smoother than silk
plenty of lipsticks staining my skin
journals with no blank spaces
novels overflowing my bookcase
*and the other, where I had nothing*

do you know which one was more fulfilling?

*THIS SECOND LAYER by Christine Jessica*

GRAVEYARD.

do I *love him to death*?

well, if he had stepped on my grave,

I would not have pulled him underneath

just to see him again,

as that would be far too greedy

I would want him to enjoy his life

without me

*with another woman*

without loss

*with newfound hope*

never longing for another me

and even being as alive instead of dead,

with red roses in my hand

at this cemetery of my heart,

I still want him to do the same

*THIS SECOND LAYER* by Christine Jessica

DO YOU HAVE ONE?

a good-looking face
must be nice to kiss

but a good-looking heart
must be nice to hold

## AN UNDERSTANDING.

I understood how to fall in love;
I lack this thing called *luster*
unless I have a man standing beside me

I understood the ocean;
I cannot find appreciation for the waves
unless I have sand on my feet

I understood the world;
I knew that everything rotates in life,
even the ground moving beneath me

I thought I understood everything -
but I still don't understand
why he was here one moment
and gone the next

*THIS SECOND LAYER by Christine Jessica*

BOW AND ARROW.

I saw you, for the first time in months

you took out a bow and arrow,
and aimed at me like I was your target

you pulled
and pulled
and pulled

until you released

*"how many events happened today*
*that made you consider living?"*

well, when you put it that way –
just this one

*THIS SECOND LAYER by Christine Jessica*

NOT WHAT I WAS PLANNING.

I was over you, I was sure of it

at least, that's what I was told

I promised myself
I wouldn't let this happen,
but here I am

with you at the end of my spine,
a cold hand on the back of my neck,
and a kiss like you were trying
to give me frostbite

*THIS SECOND LAYER by Christine Jessica*

AN EMPTY MIND. – haiku

a day will soon come

where I do not think of you

maybe a few more

*THIS SECOND LAYER by Christine Jessica*

REMAINS.

I've been thinking about
thinking about you,

should I continue
or let you fade away?

if I keep these remainders,
what will remain of me?

FROSTBITE.

I was fooled by the warmth

of your eyes,

they looked at me

so invitingly

I decided to reach my hand

into your chest

and touched the space

where your heart should be

my fingers turned pale and blue

similar to the color

of the Heaven-containing sky above

telling me, *I wish I needed you*

*THIS SECOND LAYER by Christine Jessica*

RAIN DAY.

my thoughts are like the weather

even those who study it for a living
tend to be wrong

did the wind blow you away,
or was it the rain?

## IF YOU ALLOWED.

you had asked me, *"were you in love?"*

I was unaware of what you wanted my answer to be. did you want to hear an awful truth, or an endearing lie? so, I pulled out my journal and began to draw.

I marked the bottom of the paper with an X. *"this is where I am, and always have been. I have never moved my entire life."* I made another X on the top of the paper. *"and this is your home. I made your mark a little smaller, because I'm starting to believe my heart takes up more space than yours."*

you stared at me like you had something to say, but chose not to. I made a line across the horizon of the paper. *"this is the line that you had imagined. it doesn't exist, but you think it does. you allowed it to separate us."*

I flipped over the paper and started making a continuous line across my journal, following sheet-by-sheet. you decided to speak, *"what are you doing?"*

even in the distance from your house to mine, this is the amount I could have loved you.

*"if only you had let me."*

*THIS SECOND LAYER by Christine Jessica*

OUT OF LOVE.

people tend to fall in love with me

at a fast pace,

they feel everything at once

I fill their world with color

I mend their hearts back together

I stick to my promises

I give them my all

but people tend to fall out of love with me

just as fast

*THIS SECOND LAYER by Christine Jessica*

GARDEN.

I planted seeds for you,
but you always forgot to water them

tears form,
waves crash,
so, we can't always rely on the rain

am I the flower,
and are you the dirt,

or do I have the ability
to conquer this
all on my own?

*THIS SECOND LAYER by Christine Jessica*

BEING COMPLETELY HONEST.

when I write a lot of words,
I find myself looking for you
hiding in between them

one day, I promise,

I will be able to spell *lies*
without believing everything you felt
was the truth

I will be able to spell *love*
without thinking of your voice cracking
while you'd say it back to me

*THIS SECOND LAYER by Christine Jessica*

GLUE.

I told myself,
I'd allow you to wander,
I had faith that your feet
would bring you back home

we broke unevenly when we shattered,
and that's why I knew
you still had pieces of me

you told me, you carried them with you
everywhere you went,
you didn't keep me on the counter
in the apartment you call *home*

thank you for gluing them back into place

the sound of love, once shattered,
now put together

## THIS SECOND LAYER by Christine Jessica

DANGER.

I fell in love with fire

I fell in love with the ocean

I fell in love with heights

I knew all of those things

could burn me

or drown me

or break me

but I never thought

falling in love with you

would end up with the same results

*THIS SECOND LAYER by Christine Jessica*

## TIME TO WASTE.

all it took was one kiss

for me to realize

I'd write about him forever

but all he could give me

were a few seconds

maybe his candle ran out

while mine still had a flame

and I can't do much

besides sit in this dark room

to admire

*THIS SECOND LAYER by Christine Jessica*

CALL ME. – haiku

call me in a few
when you are older and wise
and have changed your mind

*THIS SECOND LAYER by Christine Jessica*

WELL...

it was a hot, Summer day,
there in the city -
the weather made me feel like
a teabag in water

time always walked away
when I was with you,
I never thought you'd leave
the room along with it

now, I know why they put
sugar and honey in iced tea

it's far too bitter, otherwise

*THIS SECOND LAYER by Christine Jessica*

LOVE IS THE POINT.

never tired of writing,
but I want to feel my words

I give, selfless
but don't receive, selfish

how am I supposed to end
my sentences with periods
when love is the point

VACATION.

I think your heart was on vacation,
was the land as beautiful as the photos
we cut out from magazines
and pinned to cork boards?

I think your love was on leave,
did you find what you were looking for,
or were you sorry you ever went?

when the good comes back,
will it go again?

*THIS SECOND LAYER by Christine Jessica*

JUST LIKE THIS.

like the wind moving through me,

like the dense fog from the morning storm,

like the stain beneath the surface,

like the ring on my one finger,

I want our love to be just

*THIS SECOND LAYER by Christine Jessica*

UNTIL YOU LEAVE.

I don't think we can truly
be appreciative of something
until it leaves

like a baby bird flying away from the nest
like my heart when you went away in Spring
like a balloon swaying past the trees
like the sand dollar washed up from sea
like my brain when I can't remember your name

## LOVE UNDER MY BREATH.

"I've waited 29 days for this kiss."

"just round it up to one month,
it sounds more invasive."

I knew I would be stuck here forever,
this mysterious warp in time
that reminds me of what it once felt like
to have your love

I know you had only given me a daisy,
and there would be someone who hands me a field,

but, between fine lines and stolen hearts,

the answer will always be you.

*THIS SECOND LAYER by Christine Jessica*

TRUST ME, I'VE TRIED.

I'm not going to waste my time
missing a person
who no longer exists

I know you're not around
to hear my cries

but I stared at the insides of my eyelids
and pictured you
as I said goodbye to a ghost

now, there's lipstick imprints
covering my bathroom walls
like an old layer of paint

I think I had imagined you were here again

*THIS SECOND LAYER by Christine Jessica*

SLOW, AND SUDDEN.

you pick off her petals with your hands
and watch them fall to the ground,
like a rose full of thorns

slow,
sudden,
I sang myself to sleep

*he loves me,*
*he loves me not*

## YOU MIGHT'VE BEEN THE MOON.

you lit a candle inside of my heart,
and when I undressed,
I saw that it didn't burn out
when you left

I am so full of warmth,
it is getting far too hot for me
to hold it all in myself

but this candle
is only a small reminder
that I am the sun

*THIS SECOND LAYER by Christine Jessica*

FORTHCOMING.

I see you arriving

like a midnight storm,

your power is imminent

I will attempt to hide you away

in a room with no windows

but this secret called *probability*

cannot be locked up

I want to explore

to see if there is better,

but I will always run back to you

like a sprinter realizing they left their shoelaces at home

your eyes say you are *done*,

but your arms spell out *come home*

*THIS SECOND LAYER by Christine Jessica*

WOLVES.

how long do you have to stare at things,
to make them crumble,
to make them bend?

I did this to the sky,
hoping it would fall on me

or, maybe, I just want the stars
to leave me be

now, I know
why wolves howl at the moon

*it looks so much like you*

*THIS SECOND LAYER by Christine Jessica*

VACATED.

I'm eating at the place you hated
here, in the city you loved
and I don't know why my eyes
cannot stray far from the floor

I have a crush and I hate it
I have trouble feeling skin
I'm trying to keep my secrets folded in

is it weird to be infatuated with her,
to the point that she could tell
another girl once lived in your heart
but vacated

I'll be anything you want me to be,
I don't want to leave
but I don't want your synchronized sympathy

I keep coming back here,
is this my residence now?

## UNDERNEATH.

your love will be the sand
and your arms will be the water

but the sea is telling me
you'll come and go like the waves

how long will it be,
until your breath pulls me under?

*THIS SECOND LAYER by Christine Jessica*

OPENHEARTED.

a flower only blooms once,
I am a never-ending garden

and I could be there again,
underneath your feet,
drowning in my tenderness

while you water me
and watch me grow

*THIS SECOND LAYER by Christine Jessica*

NOT REAL.

he doesn't want beauty
or brains
or personality

at least, not mine

he wants magic
a princess trapped in a castle
a fairytale ending

he could have had one with me

but, if he wants a porcelain doll
to play pretend,
I will watch him

while I am here with a king

*THIS SECOND LAYER by Christine Jessica*

LEARNING.

this is how you live –

*you smile,*

*you frown,*

*you feel,*

*you don't,*

*you hope,*

*you pray,*

*you kiss,*

*you touch,*

*you want,*

*you need,*

and this is how you love.

*THIS SECOND LAYER by Christine Jessica*

THINGS I HOPE FOR.

I hope so much for you -

that you can wake up with a smile
on your face every morning,
that you treat yourself
the way you're meant to be treated,
that you don't feel so alone
because I am not there to hold

and I hope so much for me -

that I can go on
even if that means without you,
that I will learn to make
just one cup of coffee instead of two,
that I become even stronger
than I am right now

## ACKNOWLEDGEMENTS.

*thank you to Amber, Gen, Cynthia, Noah, & Nina for being the amazing people in my life. I'm so honored that I know you, and to have you to lean on.*

*thank you to Robert, Ellen, and Sue, as always, for making me believe in myself. I was never a confident person, until you showed me that I was just a turtle stuck in its shell.*

*thank you to my wonderful family, for encouraging me to continue writing and to follow my passion.*

*especially, thank **you** and anyone else who has read this book. I couldn't have done this without the tremendous amount of love and support you have given to me. I truly hope my words have helped you in whatever way you needed them to.*

*love,*

*Christine*

*xoxo*

## ABOUT THE AUTHOR.

---

*Christine Jessica is a poet who was born and raised in a small town in New Jersey. she visits New York City frequently to spend time with her friends, and plans on moving there in a few years.*

*Christine started writing poetry at the age of twelve. now, she commits to writing at least three poems a day – totaling to over 1,000 in her lifetime.*

*Christine gained readers from all over the world – including France, Germany, and the UK. her first book, Roses in SoHo, was published at the age of seventeen.*

## SOCIAL MEDIA.

*website* - www.rosesinsoho.com

*twitter* - @rosesinsoho

*instagram* - @rosesinsoho

*tumblr* – christinejessica.tumblr.com

*press/business inquiries:* rosesinsoho@gmail.com

# SOCIAL MEDIA

https://www.instagram.com

https://www.facebook.com

https://www.tiktok.com

https://discord.gg/cs-thinkroom

https://www.youtube.com/c/christianthinkroom

# INDEX.

A CHOICE (pg. 82)

A DEEP BREATH (pg. 48)

AFTER ALL (pg. 61)

ALONE, NO LONGER (pg. 43)

AN EMPTY MIND (pg. 90)

AN UNDERSTANDING (pg. 87)

A SCENE IN A COFFEE SHOP (pg. 39)

A STORM (pg. 31)

A STORYBOOK ENDING (pg. 12)

A SUN DAY (pg. 28)

AT THE TRAFFIC LIGHT (pg. 51)

BEDSHEETS (pg. 74)

BEING COMPLETELY HONEST (pg. 97)

BETWEEN (pg. 30)

BLUE SKIES ARE CALLING (pg. 36)

BOW AND ARROW (pg. 88)

BUSY STREETS, CROWDED SIDEWALKS (pg. 8)

CALL ME (pg. 101)

CAT'S CRADLE (pg. 26)

CHERRIES (pg. 21)

DANGER (pg. 99)

DEAR: WOMEN (pg 71)

DISASTER (pg. 9)

DISTANT (pg. 80)

DIVE (pg. 14)

DOPAMINE (pg. 46)

DO YOU HAVE ONE? (pg. 86)

DO YOU LOVE? (pg. 23)

DO YOU WANT TO HEAR A SECRET? (pg. 41)

DREAM WORLD (pg. 52)

EVERY LAST BIT (pg. 55)

FORTHCOMING (pg. 111)

FRANCESCA (pg. 27)

FROSTBITE (pg. 92)

GARDEN (pg. 96)

GLUE (pg. 98)

GONE, FORGOTTEN (pg. 72)

GRAVEYARD (pg. 85)

HIDE AND SEEK (pg. 66)

I AM HERE (pg. 29)

IF IT DOES (pg. 58)

IF YOU ALLOWED (pg. 94)

IN A RUSH (pg. 16)

IT ALMOST FELT LIKE LOVE (pg. 49)

IT WAS PROBABLY NOTHING (pg. 73)

I WISH IT WASN'T (pg. 63)

JUST LIKE THIS (pg. 105)

KEEP YOURS (pg. 40)

LAST SUMMER (pg. 18)

LEARNING (pg. 117)

LEILA (pg. 35)

LITTLE THINGS HURT THE WORST (pg. 13)

LIVING IN A DREAM (pg. 10)

LONG GONE (pg. 59)

LOVED (pg. 75)

LOVE IS THE POINT (pg. 103)

LOVE UNDER MY BREATH (pg. 107)

MANNEQUINS (pg. 20)

MAYBE IT WAS (pg. 24)

MAY IS HERE (pg. 7)

MY EYES (pg. 65)

NIGHT (pg. 68)

NINE P.M. (pg. 44)

NOT HEARTBROKEN (pg. 34)

NOT REAL (pg. 116)

NOT WHAT I WAS PLANNING (pg. 89)

NOW THAT YOU KNOW (pg. 67)

ONE DAY LATER (pg. 37)

OPENHEARTED (pg. 115)

ORIGAMI (pg. 56)

OUT OF LOVE (pg. 95)

POINTING TO THE SKY (pg. 38)

POSSIBILITY (pg. 54)

POWER (pg. 50)

RAIN DAY (pg. 93)

REMAINS (pg. 91)

REGRET (pg. 17)

SANDALWOOD (pg. 79)

SHOOT (pg. 64)

SKELETON (pg. 57)

SLOW, AND SUDDEN (pg. 109)

SNOWFALL (pg. 45)

SPARKS (pg. 77)

SUAD (pg. 15)

SUNSHINE (pg. 32)

TELL ME (pg. 78)

THE ANSWER WAS RASPBERRY (pg. 42)

THE KEY TO YOUR APARTMENT (pg. 83)

THE ONE WITH YOU IN IT (pg. 84)

THE WEATHER OUTSIDE (pg. 22)

THINGS I HOPE FOR (pg. 118)

THIS IS MY TURNING PAGE (pg. 62)

THIS IS WHERE I'LL LEAVE YOU (pg. 25)

THREE SUGARS, PLEASE (pg. 81)

TIME TO WASTE (pg. 100)

TRUST ME, I'VE TRIED (pg. 108)

UNDERNEATH (pg. 114)

UNTIL YOU LEAVE (pg. 106)

VACATED (pg. 113)

VACATION (pg. 104)

WATCH ME (pg. 60)

WELL... (pg. 102)

WHAT ELSE? (pg. 69)

WHAT'S STOPPING ME? (pg. 19)

WHEN (pg. 53)

WHEN FIRST LOVE ENDS (pg. 33)

WHEN LIFE HANDS YOU LEMONS (pg. 11)

WHILE YOU GO (pg. 70)

WHO ARE YOU? (pg. 76)

WOLVES (pg. 112)

YOU MIGHT'VE BEEN THE MOON (pg. 110)

YOUNG ENOUGH TO KNOW BETTER (pg. 47)

www.ingramcontent.com/pod-product-compliance
Lightning Source LLC
Chambersburg PA
CBHW022113090426
42743CB00008B/829